Lone Sail

Lone Sail

Roger Brammer

First published in 2016
by KairosTimeNow
© Roger Brammer
ISBN-13: 978-1530489725
ISBN-10: 1530489725

Dedication

To my wife Kate and son Richard
– and with thanks & love to all my family and friends, fellow
Readers and all at Stoke Minster.

In memoriam: Ric Luxton and John McGillen – gone to that
place with no horizons where Time never ends . .

And with special thanks to Father Daniel O'Leary, Victoria
Brown, the Rev'd Pauline Shelton, Howard Jones and Lindsay
Hall for helping to make this book a reality.

The cold moon is still shining John . . not forgetting the Hart
family – or my soul friend the Rev'd Maureen Tideswell.

'Nobody knows much more of this than anybody sees'
(Bob Weir – the Grateful Dead)

And thanks also to the Rev'd David Lingwood for turning me
on to the Office of Evening Prayer & showing me the spiritual
discipline of just turning up.

– And to Phil Hassall for showing me the Way and fond
memories of many walks with Mark Fowler.

Anj – keep shining thru.

"STAY HUNGRY, STAY FOOLISH"

Foreword

Over the years, I have watched Roger Brammer mature as a poet. There is now a confidence and a kind of inner authority in his writing. This is evident in the way he uses words. He waits for them, dances with them, is surprised by them. At times, it seems that they are in charge, at other times he does the leading. And we, the readers, move with the ebb and flow of the dance.

Each poem is mined from the poet's unique life and his vibrant imagination. They all have an authenticity inscribed in them; they ring with a searing honesty. They are born in the soul. They are tinged with memory, nostalgia, pathos, profound depth. They reveal hints and glimpses of a deeper mystery, unfolding layers of life.

A richness of imagination colours these pages. They attract the reader. And before you know it, the poet has silently persuaded you into that place in yourself where the emotions are hiding, with their invisible tears. And then beautiful wells called poems swell, and overflow into others creativity because we are all poets at heart. It is what makes us like God – the grace of imagination. Unknowingly, we yearn to be poets, to make shapes with words from our own beauty, to become who we are meant to be. Mary Oliver wrote:

'Poetry is a life-giving force. For poems are not words, after all, but fires for the cold, ropes let down to the lost, something as necessary as bread in the pockets of the hungry. Yes, indeed.'

As you surrender to the pull of the poems you realise that they were crafted and forged on the smithy of the poet's soul. That is why they are so powerful. In them, he blurs the distance between nature and grace, between the visible and the invisible. Unerringly he has learned the craft of incarnation. Not many are sure-footed on the ladder pitched between the ordinary and the extraordinary, between earth and heaven. Roger Brammer is. Here is one example:

our incarnate lord

the realisation of love
of a love that's – almost –
too much to bear

how it
– more precious than diamonds –
becomes as commonplace
as a mother and child
going to school,
as a mother's love and care.

as commonplace as kisses,
as everyday as breathing

and how both
are miracle:

love breaths,
fragrant love breathings

traces of God
echoes of God

everywhere
in every solitary cell

May this collection give you the holy courage to give birth to
your own poems, in your own soul.

Daniel O'Leary

Daniel O'Leary is a priest, author and speaker whose most
recent book is 'The Happiness Habit' – published by Columba
Press.

He is also a regular contributor to The Tablet.

About the Author

Roger Brammer lives in the Midlands and is a Reader in the Church of England in the Lichfield Diocese.

Contents

"There is a river whose streams make
                    glad the city of God,
the holy place of the dwelling of
                        the Most High.
God is in the midst of her;
        therefore shall she not be removed;
God shall help her at the break of day."

psalm 146

early

the seven o' clock bird
of hope and light to come,
that I've often heard before
in deepest winter, sings

as it offers up
its cheerful
possibilities

– with its little runs & trills
of uneven, cracked, scat notes:
the triples and broken up pairs
like lovers, gapped by silence,
its sudden streams
of five notes all together
pursuing some major theme
that only the sky
can really develop or ignite

– or us. 'listen'
the lone dawn bird chants
 – it can seem – 'listen,
take and make:

bless, break, share
this light that's
sure to come,
like the bread
of Christ's body,

of all that
I'm singing
out
to you

— this whole life
and world and word
that I give

this love.'

the oaks at mamre

what happens in the early morning
is in the beginning of Time . .

is the Word singing-in our life
thru the seas, stones, birds, the
reaches of land, fire.

bones dancing into thinking, seeing;
the nervous energy of being rippling
thru the wild berries and stars . .

and camping beneath the trees
that time – at Mamre – the table set
like the icon to be, the scene set
for us to enter and partake:

to eat meat and bread,
to sip the wine.
to greet strangers
and spread outwards, breed

– and to begin to dance in love
& across that fine, uncertain line
between the angels and ourselves . .

between how we are now
and how one day we will be
in and out of time,
clothed in new minds.

sol justitiae
'we are the eyes of the world' *

the sacrament,
for everything that's
– signed, pointing –
beyond us;
for everything that's
deep inside us too
– in the depths of who we are
and in the depths of where
we came and come from, issue.

deep as sheol,
high as heaven,
all the mystery of when we were, are,
and were not here;
all the mystery of God
tumbling within us
and without us
– far off and then so near.

there's protection, flight and promise
in all our ancient cells,
in all our strands of story & unknowing:
how the aimless seeming little road
springs up to greet us
and begs us to travel upon it
just once more and for the very first time.

the beauty of our moment
opens up like a flower,
the squalls and showers of rain,

the second, minute, hour.
how we wander you and I
and venture into time and love
with stars beneath, inside, above,
with all the wonder spinning out
like a planet that suddenly sees itself
hurtling on its axis

and crashing thru the big blue yonder
as it views itself in itself thru itself
hanging there as real as rock and true as love
– shining in the blackness
like the sun of righteousness
with all its light dawning in our hearts
and pouring thru it from its above.

we are, it is, as splendid as that,
see how the miracle of this attracts
all to it, forwards, back and still;
see how we shine like waves.

*Jerry Garcia

moments of grace

knowing now where we're heading to
but not how long it will take
nor precisely where it is – or isn't –
                         that we're going;
we have no stake in the temporary future somehow
– and the past is a gone zone of joy and error.

there's a thin faith, the trying of believing
– to believe but none of us knowing –
and these moments of grace
when it's enough to be here still,
to still be in it all, the life
kicking and outpouring, the nerves
jumping, the rain falling
– a dog barking down the street.

the time is gathering and glowing like coals,
our hearts beat, pulses racing ..

how it is here now, how quiet and complete
– and, at the last and least, how
we're eventually hospitable:

how we mouth our prayers
into the unknown and to the final stranger.

to a lady
'the big hurt'

your silence make me lonely,
lonesome, unappreciated;
showing how a friendship can be, forlorn,
when it's no longer
reciprocated.

all the speculations
and wonderings:
the why's and
how did this
come to pass?

the sudden excluding of love
– its peremptory
dismissal.

now in this exile
of non-communication
there's this trying
to decipher
what the silence
might be trying to say

– or what it exactly
states instead
so completely
and precisely
that there's nothing
more to be said

it is just as it is
perfect in itself.

leaving
'when you come to the land that the Lord will give you.' *

it passes over so many times it seems
but one day will drop like a four o'clock darkness
                                              in winter
as clear and clean as a religious moment;
a clarity of bright spring water in an unclear world
– is what we all hope for I guess
and not the ache and constriction of a cancer
growing into strangled effect: its bitterness, its hold,
                                    its bunched up fingers tightening.

the blood of our lives is painted on the lintels
                                          of our minds
and we watch the loveliness of the world still lit,
watch for the paschal mystery of God to spare us this,
this journeying to a far country .. not yet,
nor yet we pray, tho' we know we cannot pay or buy it off
but that it will come, as welcome we hope and
                                          not cursed; O
Lord help us, Holy Mary mother of God
pray for us sinners now and at the hour of our deaths.

a memory of a mother as she sat in the back
                                    of an ambulance
driving away that day – or the memory
of an old man sitting on a park bench
                    waiting for the swooping gulls to take him
– we are all at sea, we wait for the walls of
                    water to roll over us,
we wait for the last beat with pulses ticking.

we are old watches sold in the bazaar in the
                              bright sunlight
− of someone else's regard and attention −
as our nerves fray like leather bands
and the heaped up piles of sand wait
                    to be turned again.

* Exodus: 12.25

reading Alice Meynell in Largs
(for Daniel O'Leary)

a fret on the sea,
one lone sail in the bay
– pale, white, silent
and your words still alive
and sailing into me:
your 'loneliness in loneliness' *.

a single star engraved
on the cover of your book,
a single sail out in the bay;
we are single souls:
earthbound, frail and momentary
tho your words have, extant,
a power over the grave
'there's loneliness in loneliness'.

cut water, waves and cut leaves,
the cut pages of your book
– we are like wreaths floating
                        on the sea
and all your charms, your poems' words
within me, to rest inside of me.

alice meynell, beloved of Ruskin and Rossetti,
still talking on this seaward facing bench
on the sea front, the promenade in Largs
– her words getting clearer and more insistent
as the sea mist
burns away
into ash, confetti,

into married and marred souls

and there's a lone sail in the bay;
her yesterdays here today
—and all her time run out.

* 'there's loneliness in loneliness'
– from 'The Visiting Sea' by Alice Meynell
(Collected Poems, 1903)

old houses

death duties took away so many
– tho' you can still sometimes see
the long avenues with spaced out trees
                                             each side,
the drives going on and on
to a heap of ruined stones
or to something else now entirely –

so much of the grandeur
was hidden from view,
hidden away like the slaves
packed in boats like sacks of
                                    perishable goods
to, for, this imperishable moment
– or so their owners thought
until the times changed
and there were just too many wings
– too much space and lack of conscience
to heat, to light, to live in
darkened.

in the woods
a rumour of madness in the family,
by the railtracks
a hint of suicide.
vast stables, old loves, chinese silks,
so many paintings of family and horses,
stuffed animals in the attic rooms,
old, lingering and impossible romances
    diaried and left in the libraries
                                    and in the lurch

– and now the gift shop
and the cafe
in the dead houses that have survived
– and a little way away the church.

words

the shadow of the drop
falling, spilling over, doesn't shake the surface of things
— but it ripples in the mind, in the eyes . .

that time:
max dubois' 'quartet for flutes'
playing in the very early, brittle morning
— and attending to it;
to the movements in the air
(played somewhere from a dead, blotted score
— dots, spots, lines — but moving now to this,
from studio and disc to radioing in
to ear, to brain, to self,
to another person listening.)

being aware of being aware
—and very much alive —
and listening to this, being aware
of who I am listening to
and what I'm listening to
and of who I am, listening;

of being here
hearing

this now
— that's later words.

skins as smooth as olives
(for K.B)

skin as smooth as olives
– you, who saved me from
all my worn out ways
of barely being,
lie beside me
in the small hours

these moments never been before
these moments came to take them,
they occupy themselves so quickly
like cat licks of time
and sometimes and suddenly
can seem to lay siege
to something more spacious,
stellar, different

in these early morning hours
I'm reading and praying
– doing the jigsaw of the gospels
and wondering about how there still
                              may be
new conditions of things
and original thoughts perhaps
– whilst you are asleep upstairs
with skin as smooth as olives

and the moments, the movements
in the single shots & frames
                of the quiet night air
– those ripples on lips when thoughts
                become words or prayers –
are so fresh and silent and can seem sacred:
thoughts becoming words
pitted, black, green
dyed or natural,
extracted, held, fixed, static;
these marks on a page, these
still lives & living voices
in the room.

the air on the skin,
the hushed whispers,
the scent of your perfume.

keep listening

the peace that we pursue
perhaps we find too late
some might say
– when our lives find us out.

what we were always
seeking to find
finally finds us
it wd. appear

– like childhood.
old skin now
but a wonder again
at all the world's
breathing; how it

breathes us in and out
– and how we love
and delight

in its attentions.
how we love
and delight

in trying to find out
just what it is
that it's saying.

intimations

frail heart beating yet
and yet one day to cease

as delicate as bluebells
this thin life and light
this tremor
how the petals, the leaves shake
how they tremble

here
so incredibly

how they ripple.

we will one day
all be released like butterflies

slight wings beating the air
flying over oceans

flying over the miles . .
sipping in
the moments

slipping
in the air streams

but never falling;

as close and near
as smoke

as burning.

words (2)

these very slippery little bits of virus, things
– signifiers – that land on the ice – floe of the page
like netted fish gasping for air
hoping for someone or something
to redeem them – to place them back again
into the water and blood of another sea
or lake or mind and reading, another where;
or to hurry them across that hollow gap
that always seems to lie between us
across the page, between our minds
like the shadows that fall backward across
                                  our lives.

how they come out of mouths
and vanish into thin air,
how they get hauled in and pinned down,
tape recorded, written, sung, pictured,
gospelled, parcelled out. 'they're
all that we have' you said, one day, when
we were both nudging at despair . .

well, not quite . . but nearly:
these little bits of mind remaking
themselves like lysergic acid on the brain
trying to reveal what's hidden;
to gulp in the moments before they
– and we – give out and die.
'the medium is the message' *, our story,
MEKTOUB, 'it is written', the Word

made flesh singing thru all this our song and line
and the beginning word singing us out
and signing us in and off like Braille
thru all the trails and swirls of time . .

we are flickering flames on screens and skins
                                    and senses
as our swimming words and worlds
both reachout, touch and fail
— like some lone sail out on the horizon
tipping out of sight and anchored in the stars . .
we are melting in our summer nights
with masts bending and shimmering still
and dancing, rippling love beyond cliffs and words,
between gliding together and colliding
and flying out images & ideas like kites
                            like the spinning birds.

* Marshall McLuhan

our incarnate lord

the realisation of love
of a love that's – almost –
too much to bear

how it
– more precious than diamonds –
becomes as commonplace
as a mother and child
going to school,
as a mother's love and care.

as commonplace as kisses,
as everyday as breathing

and how both
are miracle:

love breaths,
fragrant love breathings

traces of God
echoes of God

everywhere
in every solitary cell.

idyll

coming into all of this
– sound, blue, panoply –
I scarcely knew that I'd left.

I felt that I'd come from somewhere
but cdn't quite remember
where that was
– & didn't think it was relevant anyway.

so here: the crashing waves,
the miles of carpets,
the unnamed flying things,
tastes, milk . .

it was dangerous too
and I didn't own it
and it wdn't always do
what I wanted it to do . .

and gradually I'd split
so completely away from it,
from where I'd come from
that I began to be me:

became aware of this and of other quiet still things
and started to look at other beings and happenings
and for that space where I might, cd. fit
– and to where I cd. walk then run.

after sleeping I, it, the creation of the world
wd. begin all over again too

and I knew I'd been here always
but where was it leading, reaching out to?

the cotswold stone, the yellow sun,
the river running under the trees,
the green willow, the roadways
it was all so old yet just begun ,
all so in place yet on the run
— and how the heart was beating.

how the breath was breathing
as it all rushed in:
the leaves rustling, the named birds singing,
the stars twinkling in the big black,
the thrill of eyes seeing

— farther away and closer in,
farther away and nearer to home,
the bright white sunlight on the stone.

waiting

cupping his heart in his right hand
he listens to the silence,
listens to the pressure bearing down all around;
outside there is a light snow falling
– already gathered into blankets on dustbin lids
and across the windows and on the roofs of silent metal
                                                    cars.

feeling the heart beat thru the skin,
listening to how muffled the sounds are in the street –
listening to the silence and waiting ,
the whole world is love-sick he suddenly things,
the whole world is waiting as it fills and shrinks.

there are procedures put in place
precisely for this waiting:
prayers, a pot of tea, a book, a radio,
a boiled egg, an entire daily office;
there are newspapers to scream out the news
and stream out the opinions of others who wait.

amidst the fruit and the dates of an afternoon,
before the dusk comes fully into being night
a lone bell rings out for Evening Prayer
                              – inside the mind –
and he gathers up his heart and hand
to wait amongst the statues and remembering tiles
to pray for those who wait.
a lit candle, two readings from the book,
a psalm and canticle, the night gathering round.
balm. a sudden smell of hair. the heart beating still

— still beating, still beating from early to late,
from now to now, from wait to wait.

doing the rounds

the peace can go at any second,
at any piece or point of time
– like a pin pulled from a grenade;
so too joy it would appear
can become compulsive too:
habitual and then shrugged off
in some Christian named confession
tho' its condition changed.

the metanoia of all our days
might yet suffice – the drawing back
into where we came, emerged
from, before all this madness
                          happened;
there a quiet music
playing in our hearts.

in the mind of Christ it gets composed
and it sings in the arms of God
who never – ever – lets us go
tho' we find it so hard
– making difficult simplicity –
to do the same . .

there where we came from
and return to, let go of finally,
we begin and once more
make new and start again.

across the lake

the fisherman on the other bank
— the further shore—
is smoking thru the time,
occasionally reeling in & baiting
                    his hook again
before casting it out and away from him
like some repented – of or unwanted sin
— tho' connected by that
fine thread, line, strong too

and I'm smoking as well thru these moments
                    of time rippling by
as the rain falls
between us
like a curtain.

jean genet tells of when, on a train once,
he met the gaze of a fellow passenger
— and, as their eyes locked,
how he felt himself becoming
who and what he was looking into
. . and vice versa.

so across the lake between us
and in that hollow space
the fisherman and I
see ourselves each
in the other perhaps

and return our separate-seeming selves
to each other to become our selves again

thru being, seeing other —an other —
and who we are;

that sharing of our lot
and of what each of us is not
— but is.

where we come from

the sky is glass
reflecting us before it breaks
and shatters into shards;

little bits of our activity, our movements
– full of God and holy night –
hold static as secrets
and fall to the ground
as if frozen

– all our bids for love
falling, dropping
like dead birds.

here is a glade of a wood
where – sometimes – if you're very quiet
you can see deer emerge from trees
like ghosts from a mist,

here where you can see them sniff
the air and check out their fear
to see if it's real or not or near:

the chastening of our lives
and our own ghosts too
from those who made us
and who yet invade the scheme of things . .
how amazingly free we are,
redeemed by our ordinary, busy little
happinesses and joys
full of love and light and concern

– but burnt and still locked in to that
depression of a war-torn father
still shell shocked by reality and by
                         the ugly spilling of blood
and by the forlorn anxiety of his wife waiting
to give you, us birth;
how we are all turned by that,
how we turn and return,
are returned.

marsha

long time ago now
riding with marsha
in a horse-drawn cab:

downtown Herat
looking for a connection,
sticky little discs
of black opium gum
like 45s, like singles.

kissing in the cab
while my girlfriend
was back in the hotel room
— the illicit thrill of that

as marsha told me
of the party they'd thrown
— her flatmate and herself —
in New York
and how nobody came

and her nervous laugh at this
and then the kiss,
her long hair, her Jewishness,
her sad sensuality . .

and sometimes it seems that
we're still riding in that cab
with the blankets drawn
over our legs, our knees

still scoring drugs
and time and
being both unfaithful
and faithful.

the rain at dawn

walking out into
the shiny gift of rain
– giving thanks
for its freshness,
for its refreshment

going to the margins and the borders of the zones,
along the peripheral, sideways road always leading,
winding back . . sounds of starlings
and distant dawn raids somewhere, the moorings
breaking open like that and the law getting imposed,
public boundaries to private lives no longer private;
there is no exemption, no diplomatic
immunity here, no ruins or safe houses
just lost and losing lives with
no story to tell;
how people go missing, underclassed, crossed out –.

rail lines, big – vast – warehouses of the mind,
the memory track of a canal trickling thru the stale, static air,
lorries sleeping in their dawn logistics,
sweating in their loads,
hoping to hook up

church steeples exploding on the horizons

– and still the rain and the lovely
little diamonds of it
landing on the black bin bags
making love and curves, swathes in the air
as the wind hits making arabesques.

there is a freedom in empty black wet roads
with the odd, infrequent cars' tyres squishing
like petals opening up

and the waiting, sheltering, huddling
as the rain greases it all:

its smear across eyes and headlights

the sodden clothes
like vagrants' rags, thieves' frayed coats,
like damp, criminal love.

—7th January, 2016, any inner city I guess . .

going back home

we are out of this world,
blind painters painting light,
we're a dream of who we are
dreaming of big visions,
of good and open and honest people
& the generous ones now dead:

their bodies found on busy commons
tucked away in hedgerows
where only dogs wander
with all the traffic circling
and no news leaking out.

we are tiny poems
like the pools of water
young children
jump up and down in,

the quirky hurdy-gurdy
playing on . .

there's a promise of chestnuts,
of toast and marshmallows
later on, a fire
in a hearth

in a house somewhere
– maybe even the promise of stories

somewhere that we
    vaguely remember
and look forward to:

that house, warmth
home then
– that knew us
& was known way back when
and is imminent and coming again
  maybe and maybe not

strung in our prayers like beads
passing thru our fingers,
like dreams out of earshot.

elegy

running out of time now
like sand in an hour glass,
the May Queen in the summer lane
seems such a long way away
across the fields

those boys
– young men with dreams –
in the meadows . .

the stolen smoke
in the woods
at the turning
that day

the glance backwards
at something happening
in the dead centre
of the village
at burning noon

all those ceremonies
and first kisses

– and making that final journey,
along the ridge and up the hill
to where we came from,

to that lit fire
in the grate,

to all the remembered voices
and starry skies,
with the hills
crowding in
all around us.

winter solstice

the sun standing still
endless seeming night
the birth of the Word
in a baby

this attempt
to put things right
to integrate our shadows
tho' it's getting late

there's hardy holly
spartan
and we make
our little shrines,
the lone chorister
singing in
the iconic moment.

'It's a Wonderful Life'
– and I still cry
at Zou-Zou's petals
and at how the wooden ball
on the stair rail
comes off in James Stewart's hand,
at Capra's warning & critique;

and we are all still
seeking you, Lord
and waiting to be found

— as the fires shine
and burn all around
like angels.

christmas mourning

as bleak as it can be, drear,
the graves, the drizzling rain,
a single rose lain by a headstone
'peacefully sleeping',
a wreath tied around a grave
with string.
the little bones that lie
to rise in glory,
waiting, dying into new life.

we celebrate the birth of Christ this day
— on this day that's always different from the rest:
a different charge & different seeming atoms even
in the structure of things, bricks

the light shining in the darkness
— un-put-out-able;

the rain sweeping across
the fields and tracks,
the meetings, phone-calls, texts.
trying to put the pieces back together again,
the remembered lines, lives and story,
the kaleidoscopic image whole
and not fragmented —repaired;
time's music heard again perhaps.

with Jesus in the manger
and angels' songs all around him
and the glory of the Lord shining thru

all the bare, spare trees,
the wires, thorns, briars

—and all the stone angels
looking down
on the paths.

lo and behold

the grace is in the lostness;
in the losing and the failing
is our saving grace

– it wd. appear, unseen
   perhaps, wd, seem.

fele, touch, the darkness,
bracket the silence

know by not knowing
care by not caring
try by not trying:

to feel our way
into our selves

seamlessly

by forgetting;

not to re-member
but just to hope:

to find out what
is already there,

to find out
what's already
therein, within.

and that we are
more than we think,

freer than we think.

JOB
(for Mike Shaw)

the orphan boy in the snow
has nowhere left to go
−except back into the cruelty .

he's shipped out, like cargo
to apple boughs,
to the fragrant scent of apples,
to orchards and good health,
to glad days and good cheer
and then to the apple towns
where his redeemer liveth.

listening to Handel now
he remembers back
− he knows his scripture

and as the bus
nears the cathedral
he find himself
inheriting the earth;

full, filled up, complete
with all the snows melted,
all the cold gone.

autumn

sound of the geese
getting ready to go
— like the day
the swallows spun in.

windfall apples
on the ground,
early silhouettes
        of night
cutting the day out
like scissors;

later the mornings
quicker the dusks

— summer's leavings.

the messages of fallen leaves
like lovers' notes
strewn around
— reminders;

October
our dreaming

the Slopes
the turnings.

winter

fast in the winter now,
it is dying;
ash laden.

looking for the catch
to release it,
to rush it out & spring an escape
from the wastes.

but for now
– deep in –
a resentment of starving birds,
threat of snows
rain across the eyes and feet

– this road to easter
with all its lenten trappings.

dreams of blossom in the mind's eye,
of promenades & summer, of avenues
and trees and love & milk & childhoods.

we're seeds trapped in the earth ,
in the soiled, bandaged graves of the dead
hoping to find the gospel truth outside us.
we're wrapped up in the possibility of ourselves

coming out again upwards into
blue skies and heaven,

of emerging from all the grey canals,

from the murk & the mud of tow-paths,
from the dull estates of houses and minds

into clear fields, the swan on its nest again,
the timing green shoots

—12th January, 2016
(i.m david bowie. 1947-2016)

at the art gallery *

Buchanan Street, wet, crowded,
a descending; so many people
unmade, undone, as in Dante.

at the art gallery: a riot
of colours and sculptures
    that amaze us; the polyester resin
that she used to make them
killed her.

she left these living tho'
to say that life cd. be good,
that devils and demons cd. be overcome
and 'Look, see the joy here'
    – she seems to implore;
the joy of life and living.

outside the rain still drizzles
and there are very rich & very poor,
a band is busking and an old guy
    begs in a doorway.

*** Glasgow Museum of Modern Art
(an exhibition of sculptures by Nikki de Saint Phalle)**

the crying shames
(for R.N.L)

waiting for you on that day, a Friday,
    to arrive
– then saying goodbye in a country pub's
                         dusk-filled car park
(with the gift of a small wooden Cross:
    'it's the Spirit of Truth' I said
    'Wow' you replied)

and in between:
a day out at York Races,
meeting for a coffee in Leek
    and walking around Buxton,
'It's romantic' you said of the Spa town
'Don't you think it's romantic?'
– and we even, for old times' sake,
smoked a little weed
and played neil young loud
              in the Hire Car
'Good songs' you said,
I concurring.

but I never saw you again
and now you are gone for good
'Eternal life or not?' I asked,
'The bone yard' you responded.

Our good song had its ending
– or will we meet again
out there where there's no horizons,
struck by grace?

on the waterfront

the church is built on this morning:
in the mist before the sun has fully come,
in the running figures of Salome and Joanna,
in the carrying of spices for the anointing
                                    to be done;
the two Mary's walking, waiting,
the sun coming up.

And here on the beach the meal,
the little fish, the charcoal fire, smoke,
the welcoming home of sailors.

And we sail on while our hearts
                              are beating
and we are filled up with your love,
with the bread, water, wine;
the little fish glide in and out
          like thoughts

inside, out
      of Time.
You can almost taste them.

And beyond the nets
the sun coming up,
this rising,
this being raised up;
everything.

'nothing except jesus christ and him crucified' *

'the seed is all we need' you said,
'the kingdom will grow itself
                        in our hearts'
– such relief at those words.

back then, in the streets behind reality,
we lived on the scraps of these days,
picked around the drugs and the garbage,
threw a little music in the mix
and focussed on our sexuality;
tripped out, came back, tripped up,
kept on travelling, found our home
    in addictions, even marched a little
to complain, to demonstrate.
we were looking for free money
the alchemy of changing loss to gain,
the alchemy of turning our sorrow and pain
into orgasms and highs, into new
    fortresses of capital
: to become rich beggars –

And they called you a 'spermologus'
– a seed picker, a scavenger,
a dealer in old, outdated ideas
– but you stuck to your guns:
'for I resolved to know nothing
while I was with you except
Jesus Christ and him crucified.'

And that seed once planted
takes its chances true,

it can even be lost to me and to you
– but I've found it hard to uproot
once it starts growing
its extravagant harvest;
how it is here now
in these arrived and waiting days.
anxieties, anxiety, confident.

* 1. Cor. 2. 1-5.

on the road
'these men who have turned the world upside down' *

in Thessalonica the peacocks
        strutting in the park,
we passed the days reading novels,
        an aircraft-carrier came into the bay –
talking to the American officers
        and reading Mrs Dalloway
the hours elapsed, collapsed
        one into the other;

then you met Damaris ,
you'd swapped books,
you gave her Diane di Prima's
        Memoir of a Beatnik
and she gave you
        Stranger in a Strange Land
which blew you away.

Later in Athens
we met her again
– she'd changed –
she rapped about these guys
who'd turned the world about.

She talked about something
   that we completely ignored
it wasn't in the game plan
it didn't figure –

It was years further
                    down the road
that I remembered Damaris
– you no longer living with me
but she, vivid in the memory,
reminding me of what I'd found,
of who had found me, in the mind,
her echoes,
the silent voice of God calling.

* Act 17.6

magnificat

this bringing into Time,
this mothering;
you are 'anawim'
– the poor of God –
singing this Pop Song
that becomes your theme
– and ours too.

those Babylonian
blues songs,
field hollers,
were your tradition
and where you came from
– are coming from –
and they're still your
–and our – mission;
yours and ours:
the Incarnation is
always here and now.

from above and sent
you lean and leant
into your fertile joy,

riffing the air;
as we sing your Protest Song
too and still,
and hear it echoing
in all our responses
– in all our responses
– in our good and in our ill –

in all of our political
works, words, worlds.

early
'they that go down to the sea for the Lord'

struggled, silent until You,
forever gazing across sea and desert landscapes;
peering into rock pools for a glimpse of what?
of myself, of clouds, of heaven?
I was very alone here seeing You only
    at evening, as evening fell, at twilight.
long restless nights making love to the ground.
mornings that came without a sound, light
rubbing out darkness, a thought of wading
into the sea, no longer to be so earth-bound;
the full gravity of the situation
occurring in cracks and rumbles, volcanic,
lonely, lonely, lonely
no bird song yet.

then you that day, that night, that
dawn, that dusk of love and eating,
that wedding feast of you being there, that
first dawn of watching you waking;
birds were singing, flying, winging
– and You had made me this.
As we walked in the evening
You gave me my tongue, bid me
name this desiring, these fruits,
these creatures, this life, this wife,
   this conversation

You looked contented
in the long grass, in the suddenly storied meadows,
You my Lord and friend and Creator.

stars, comets, blinking.
We looking for You, longing for You.
You looking at the flowers.
You dying for us.
You dying for us.
roar of the seas in the mind,
in the eye.

wanting

something bigger
than my small self
to belong to
to long for

to be with;

a part of
and not
apart from
all this life
that's rushing
thru a life.

to marry
these up:

the heart beat
and what
the eye sees
the eye sees:

this strange world
that's outside me
and always beyond me
tho' mirrored

and my
divided self

looking on
and in.

comes a time

comes a time
when only God
can give you
what you want

– what you desire
& what you need –

and all you
will want then
will be God

– and this
is why
perhaps
we pray

will pray
some day
be fed

now
and forever.

now
and at the hour
of our deaths

now
and at the hour
of being born

translated.

joanna

in bristol one night:
heavy black hash
and a crazy guy
tripping in a room.

we were remembering
a death I remember:
a suicide that
connected us all.

I recall too
that we made it together,
me and you, you and I so high
and in the morning
you gave me a bracelet
with your name engraved
upon it

– and I toyed with that
with my fingers
on the bus
that drove out of town.

and I knew then that I was
toying with love again
and you stayed with me
inside my head for a while.

now all these years later
those days return and intrude:
joanna, the flat and the room,

the hash and the acid and incense
and even her, your, perfume.

going back

seem to be going
back to becoming
the boy I used to be

– feeling as I
remember he felt,
seeing a world
& figuring it out

– as he both
did and didn't –

and thinking about
those old photographs,
those stills in my mind

and knowing that
I, too, will soon
become a ghost
like the people there:

in the beach scenes
with the donkeys
and the smiles
and the ice creams

– with all
the frozen waves.

lone sail
'sail on, sail on sailor' *

thru the night watches,
cars' lights cornering on ceilings
until birth and those first
faltering steps
– and then the sudden lurch
into anxiety.

boy in the mizzen mast
floating cold
and the ship sailing on . .
the boy, this boy
comes to himself;
he's no longer beached
wrecked
but running.

those postage stamps
that he once collected
he now travels,
scraps of these days
unravelling in his mind
like travellers' tales;

back of the mind
back of a world
back of the world
and sentenced to
certain trips

— and all by himself
in a lifetime.

*Brian Wilson

chestnut street
(for Ric)

those 5 o'clock phone calls
on Sundays via Skype,
from Chestnut Street
in a town in Massachusetts

– when I never knew
quite what to say because
I still hadn't found
the 'me' that I was after

– hadn't located myself at all
and now I'd give almost anything,
almost anything & everything
to hear your voice again

(with me a little nearer
to myself again and now
– and hitting the mark more closely
tho' further from the pain)

but with you
–senor, compadre –
gone away, shifted
entirely to that place

with no horizons.
that place or zone
that's out of time & range
– with no ways or means

for us to link up with
or to answer or to home in on
or transmit; no ways
to get it across and no means

to get across it now either
(both the usual tensions and that gap
between us that's different
from an ocean or a sea) – only dreams.

**—in memoriam: Richard Neil Luxton
(1950-2010)**

dust
(i.m P.H)

1) going to the funeral

travelling to an old friend's funeral,
the train to Euston moving like a silver dart,
    a knife cutting thru fields shrouded in mist;
an overwhelming feeling of weakness
– of the fragility of our being here still alive,
                                        still quick.

black winter overcoat,
white shirt, black jacket, black tie
    rolled up in the jacket's pocket
and coiled, ready to unravel and tie itself
    for a eulogy; the reckoning of the event
– of old peer group friends gathered, the woollen scarves
and leather gloves and none of this attire sufficing
    to cover up what is actually within:

which in my case is an anxious, quite scared man
who still clothes me from the inside out,
from the outside leading in to the one who's
                            still a boy
whistling in the dark; and who, nervous, on edge,
looks at the fast fields and trees passing by
    so quickly, so incredibly quickly

like my friend, lying dead in the chapel,
like you and I, like us.

2) at the funeral

there's a misty but still vivid orange sun
sinking into the boughs of the trees at
                          the far end of our vision,
sinking into the Cross and all that's nailed to it
our corruption, our dissolution and our deaths;
a Chelsea Football Club flag is draped over the coffin
and there's an other-worldly hope of sorts,
– but for how long will that be, is that?
does the memory stay preserved like a chain letter
or by some apostolic succession?
there's a certain winter glow in us
but is that only cold comfort
for the one who's gone, the one who's dead?

the prayers and the mentions of God
are post-Christian and almost apologetic . .

it's a plain chapel, small, intimate,
packed out with black cab drivers
and a smattering of old hippies
together with the small, precious
kernel of the immediate family.
two sons help carry the coffin in,
tears, eulogies and Joe Cocker singing
'With a little help from my friends'
then Pink Floyd and out

– to the gloaming; sun now set and gone.
the friend, husband, work-mate, father, story
has passed on and the curtains are drawn;
outside in the grounds there are instructions

and directions as to where we'll meet up
– end up, later on.

Putney Vale Cemetery,
November 2014.

nothing falling after all
'evening passed and morning came' *

moment by moment
in our sight
can we bear to lose
this stellar night?

will it well up
within us
in our flight?
is it all inside us
anyway
this tender dawning,
drowning
of the day?

this light
this dust that we are,
our travelling to
the furthest star.

nothing falling
    after all
here we are suspended:

and in the garden
our kind God
walking
hand in hand
with us

– as all the mornings

and evenings,
all the seasons,
chances
and discoveries emerge,
come out,
ignite.

*Genesis 1.5

mary
for Pauline Shelton

Mary truly incredible
it cannot be
– so let it be.

Mary, missing, silent
then full,
full of
amazing poetry.

Mary,
your sisters
love
and affirm you.

You are
'The Wretched of the Earth' *
you are;
all who are made mute,
all who are silenced.

In the house of bread
you pour out
your love for us,
our love for us
– and at Cana
you instruct your son.

Mary, Mary
pray for us Mary
now and at
the hour of our birth;

now and at
the hour of our
– releasing –
death.

* Frantz Fanon

lone sail (2)
'a seaboy on the giddy mast'

the poor boy
who sails the sea
can never get free
not really

that boy in the mizzen mast
floating cold
and all at sea and callow

that poor little boy
looking down at the sea
and at all the sky above him

– at the nothing
wrapped around him
and who is cold.

it gets chill up there
as he tugs his thoughts
around that self
that is all that
he really owns,
as he ties them tight
like string around a coat

and as he prays that
God is with him or inside him
– the Mothers of Sorrows
in the stars
or on the horizon

being scanned for

and he becoming, merging,
as one part or spar
−or limb − of the crucifix
the mast, his mast,
is making:

building the machinery
of Time
as he huddles against
the rain.

lone self, lone sail
sailing from here
to back again

to further along the coast

and being called
into deep water,
from all the wild seas
and foreign harbours
home.

* John Clare

the thrush singing suddenly

the thrush singing suddenly
   in the winter dark
before the slow dawning of the day.
The rush of notes urge, surge, to
break in light thru sound almost
and hopefully; a bringing in
and come what may. 'And light
it must surely be' is what I hear it say
— tho' the dark continues long after
   the song's ending but the singing, the notes
remain, are still here in memory;
those notes falling thru mind and air
like cracks in ice, like meltwater.

Scant little song, a meiosis,
but something more in it somehow.
Body and soul the whole incarnation
   of the day to come and already begun
in the throat and the beak of the bird
—in its soundworld and dripping notes,
in its almost-words and sung song:
'and light it must surely be';
sarx egeneto *
hymning, singing
bird flesh.

* 'and the word became flesh' – John 1. 14

lovers and friends

we run so far away
from one another
and ourselves

and yet there is still
that yearning to be
with each other

sometimes the charms
of love are so fresh
and unexpected
that we want to
uncover them
and reveal them
to our separate selves

to tell ourselves
to others and
let others
tell themselves

to see the
actual beauty
of our lives

and lie naked
together loving
each the other;

that way of seeing:
to embrace intimately

that intimacy
of how and who
we are and of

who and where
we meet – and
when and why.

the start of summer

the start of summer
is the First Test at Lords
with the French Open and the Derby
just around the corner,

is towards the end of May
is Mary's time −,

is how the early mornings
are suddenly so light, so day

and how the evenings linger;

bluebells everywhere,
a dazzling brilliance,
an emoticon.

our listening hearts . .
(for Merry Evans)
'heart speaks unto heart' *

our listening hearts . .
the listening heart of each one of us
   listening to the heart of God
in the silence of ourselves,
in our helplessness;

here where our God,
our Lord
is helpless too

– and in that,
from that, is
how S(He) helps us
to love.

the pitch of the sound
heard silently,
perhaps a flower
or a bird seen,

a butterfly
– a slight, trembling
alighting to sip;

a wave is the sea.
pulses . .

* Blessed John Henry Newman

still time
'Time is that which ends"

the more that we do
the more time gets away from us
and the less that we do
the more it fills itself out

time's elasticity:
how it's perceived
as it's passing,

how
it spills
thru our
hands

and minds

as we
breathe it
in and out

– and that
kairos moment
before the two,
in between,
and after,

that pause
in the meantime

— that isn't
mean at all

just still;

not stillborn
but still
to become
to be

and only
later some time
to cease.

*** William S Burroughs (The Final Academy – programme
notes)**

end of the road
'I will never disown you' *

all the meals
with all those sinners
in ports and
little courtyards,

the tacked up messages
on youth hostel notice boards

the new wine

farewells and meetings
in soukhs and bazaars
spirit to material to spirit

STRANGER IN A STRANGE LAND

mint tea
and
kif,

the black existential
   uniforms
and
forbidden drugged
fruit . .

all those signs
and allusions:

to a start of something
in the fresh spray
of the sea
over the harbour wall

to the Beat Hotel
in Rue Gît-le-Cœur –

to the tender cut throats
and young massive
almost infinite
lungs
and
colour suddenly colour
and portable lives & tape recorders

– and all of us falling from our faith
and drinking in again the Kingdom of God
but not until . .

those joyful meals remember?
your coming back to us once more Lord
raised again to wonder
and all of us here waiting for and on you
– to be taken up into you –
and wandering around ourselves in the zones now
in the gardens of the Alhambra, in Thessalonika
                                        or Algiers, wherever . .

this
waiting thru
over

to begin again

* Mark 14.31

to hold us in his love

waiting on God in the silence of our hearts,
asking, seeking, knocking on the door of reality:
opening it and walking thru it into God,
into the fullness of our lives.

old souls, new fruit, being found,
living on holy ground, the fire burning;

look. see. only today,
pray now in this moment, in this instant,
give everything for the pearl of great price
& then when you have it give it too away:

in love, in being, in seeing
how our God has come

and clothed himself within us

− and us in this naked loss of shame
living on and in the fresh air of God, his fragrance.

figuring, emptying ourselves out
to him, to realise
our selves −

to breathe him in as he
breathes us out

to hold us in his love
to hold our hearts beating
to hold our beating hearts . .

to sail on in him
even when they and we
have, are beaten:

the wind, the very breath of God
still, yet, blowing thru our minds and sails.

we haven't time

(1)

we haven't time
only the warm lights
– sanctuary, home, intimacy –
of the houses across the backs . .
just – and this much more
than enough in time, in fact –
the quiet watches of prayer:
that being with our God who is within us too
the pearl of great price
in the very early morning
before we get tuned into by a world
and turned and relocated by our minds.

we've the flow of moments
as they arrive and then track back,
the arriving time, instants that pass thru us
for a good long while yet, relentless –
and a short, brief time too

and the loose change
– and again: more than enough –
of hope and love.

our pockets of resistance
are all emptied out in the end it's true
but we have our Lady, the Lady of Pity
there to attend to us, to be with us
then in that end that just might be
a beginning, another beginning

– or a going on and
back to where we came from
in the very first place
before we got torn & turned out,
before we were dispelled and born.

(2)

and in the yards
a few flowers
and stuff thrown out:

wild flower seeds,
an old settee,
the sunlight glinting thru

the ghosts
and present cats.

telegraphs poles, wires,
windfall apples,
lives, birds

– and all the time
in the world
hanging loose, dropping, falling
or stretched – tight, taut –

breaking thru . .
not much time left perhaps.

travelling man
'ad personalitatem requiritur ultima solitudo' *

there is a man, middle-aged on a boat
in a photograph; in this image of a boat
of the boat, arms resting on the rail,
looking towards the farther shore in the distance
that's away from him, beyond him, out of touch & reach –

he is examining his thoughts perhaps:
looking out to recover them from within his head,
from within his mind to form a relationship
–or he is thinking back to himself, relaying
what he receives from his eyes,
the vision, their vision, eyes as theories, sight's icon.

he is looking out,
he is looking in,
both perhaps,
simultaneously
in silence.

it's an old photograph in black and white,
a hint of brown, daguerrotype, sepia.

the chop of the sea
as the boat ploughs thru
suggests movement
as movement there surely was

but imaged in the old snap
the sea and the man

are still and immobilised
as is the small settlement of houses
across the way from him like God.

so he looks out now and forever, imagining,
at where he's travelled to or back
to where he's come from, is leaving,
as the Father pours Himself out into the Son
and the Son returns, gives, it all back to Him
– the Spirit without limit

or maybe he's just looking across and sideways
at what his journey passes,
at what his life passes thru, is passing or being passed thru,
at what he's passing on.

* Duns Scotus
('that which makes man a person is radical solitariness')

to rest my heart

to rest my heart
now and when
I lie down to sleep

to rest it from
the vivid colours,
from the sound
of energetic violins
or all the instruments
that can scratch awake
the morning and
pour out its sun
to peel the day open
and bathe my skin

there is an ancient room
with rocking horse,
with mother and cradle
that I can never
go back to again
tho' it lives a little
inside me in a newsreel of days

there: where and when
my heart beat savagely and wildly
and there was little need
to be still but only to enjoy;
there and now it is all locked up,
knocked down, refurnished by strangers
or lying derelict

. . and now I have to go
sooner than I think or know
away into You
who once gave me this

the father's look, the mother's kiss
the young and skipping beats of love.

– Ash Wednesday, 2016

Printed in Great Britain
by Amazon